Immigration to the United States

Mexican Immigrants

Richard Worth

Robert Asher, Ph.D., General Editor

Facts On File, Inc.

Immigration to the United States: Mexican Immigrants

Facts On File, Inc.
132 West 31st Street
New York NY 10001

Library of Congress Cataloging-in-Publication Data
Worth, Richard.
  Mexican immigrants / Richard Worth.
    p. cm – (Immigration to the United States)
  Includes bibliographical references and index.
  ISBN 0-8160-5690-0
  1. Mexican Americans–History–Juvenile literature. 2. Immigrants–United States–
History–Juvenile literature. 3. Mexican Americans–Juvenile literature. I. Title. II. Series.
  E184.M5W675 2005
  304.8'73072–dc22

2004014302

Facts On File books are available at special discounts when purchased in bulk quantities for businesses, associations, institutions, or sales promotions. Please call our Special Sales Department in New York at (212) 967-8800 or (800) 322-8755.

You can find Facts On File on the World Wide Web at http://www.factsonfile.com

Cover design by Cathy Rincon
A Creative Media Applications Production
Interior design: Fabia Wargin & Luís Leon
Editor: Laura Walsh
Copy editor: Laurie Lieb
Proofreader: Tania Bissell
Photo researcher: Jennifer Bright

Photo Credits:
p. 1 © CORBIS; p. 4 © CORBIS; p. 11 © Getty Images/Hulton Archive; p. 15 © Bettmann/CORBIS; p. 20 © Getty Images/Hulton Archive; p. 19 © Getty Images/Hulton Archive; p. 23 © Bettmann/CORBIS; p. 26 © CORBIS; p. 32 © Bettmann/CORBIS; p. 37 © CORBIS; p. 39 © Bettmann/CORBIS; p. 43 © Bettmann/CORBIS; p. 45 © CORBIS; p. 47 Library of Congress/America Memory Collection; p. 48 © CORBIS; p. 51 Library of Congress/America Memory Collection; p. 57 © Bettmann/CORBIS; p. 59 © Bettmann/CORBIS; p. 63 © Charles Jean Marc/CORBIS SYGMA; p. 64 © Time Life Pictures/Getty Images; p. 67 © Associated Press Photo; p. 69 © Bettmann/CORBIS; p. 71 © Alain Nogues/CORBIS SYGMA; p. 72 © Associated Press Photo; p. 74 © Associated Press Photo; p. 77 © Tom & Dee Ann McCarthy/CORBIS; p. 80 © AP Photo/Ira Schwartz; p. 82 © CORBIS SYGMA; p. 84 © Peter Turnley/CORBIS; p. 87 © Reuters/CORBIS

"I Am Joaquín" by Rodolfo "Corky" Gonzales is reprinted with permission from the publisher of *Message to Aztlan* (Houston: Arte Público Press–University of Houston, 2001.)

Printed in the United States of America

VH PKG 10 9 8 7 6 5 4 3 2 1

This book is printed on acid-free paper.

Previous page: *A young Mexican-American woman takes part in a 1971 rally against discrimination in Sacramento, California.*

Contents

A Nation
of Immigrants

Robert Asher, Ph.D.

Left:
*Young Mexican
Americans gather
in Los Angeles in
June 1943 at the
end of a week of
rioting sparked by
racial tensions
between Mexican
Americans and
Anglos.*

Human beings have always moved from one place to another. Sometimes they have sought territory with more food or better economic conditions. Sometimes they have moved to escape poverty or been forced to flee from invaders who have taken over their territory. When people leave one country or region to settle in another, their movement is called emigration. When people come into a new country or region to settle, it is called immigration. The new arrivals are called immigrants.

People move from their home country to settle in a new land for two underlying reasons. The first reason is that negative conditions in their native land push them to leave. These are called "push factors." People are pushed to emigrate from their native land or region by such things as poverty, religious persecution, or political oppression.

The second reason that people emigrate is that positive conditions in the new country pull them to the new land. These are called "pull factors." People immigrate to new countries seeking opportunities that do not exist in their native country. Push and pull factors often work together. People leave poor conditions in one country seeking better conditions in another.

Sometimes people are forced to flee their homeland because of extreme hardship, war, or oppression. These immigrants to new lands are called refugees. During times of war or famine, large groups of refugees may immigrate to new countries in

search of better conditions. Refugees have been on the move
from the earliest recorded history. Even today, groups of
refugees are forced to move from one country to another.

Pulled to America

For hundreds of years, people have been pulled to America
seeking freedom and economic opportunity. America has
always been a land of immigrants. The original settlers of
America emigrated from Asia thousands of years ago. These first
Americans were probably following animal herds in search of
better hunting grounds. They migrated to America across a land
bridge that connected the west coast of North America with
Asia. As time passed, they spread throughout North and South
America and established complex societies and cultures.

Beginning in the 1500s, a new group of immigrants came
to America from Europe. The first European immigrants to
America were volunteer sailors and soldiers who were promised
rewards for their labor. Once settlements were established, small
numbers of immigrants from Spain, Portugal, France, Holland,
and England began to arrive. Some were rich, but most were
poor. Most of these emigrants had to pay for the expensive
ocean voyage from Europe to the Western Hemisphere by
promising to work for four to seven years. They were called
indentured servants. These emigrants were pushed out of
Europe by religious persecution, high land prices, and poverty.
They were pulled to America by reports of cheap, fertile land
and by the promise of more religious freedom than they had in
their homelands.

Many immigrants who arrived in America, however, did
not come by choice. Convicts were forcibly transported from
England to work in the American colonies. In addition,

thousands of African men, women, and children were kidnapped in Africa and forced onto slave ships. They were transported to America and forced to work for European masters. While voluntary emigrants had some choice of which territory they would move to, involuntary immigrants had no choice at all. Slaves were forced to immigrate to America from the 1500s until about 1840. For voluntary immigrants, two things influenced where they settled once they arrived in the United States. First, immigrants usually settled where there were jobs. Second, they often settled in the same places as immigrants who had come before them, especially those who were relatives or who had come from the same village or town in their homeland. This is called chain migration. Immigrants felt more comfortable living among people whose language they understood and whom they might have known in the "old country."

Immigrants often came to America with particular skills that they had learned in their native countries. These included occupations such as carpentry, butchering, jewelry making, metal machining, and farming. Immigrants settled in places where they could find jobs using these skills.

In addition to skills, immigrant groups brought their languages, religions, and customs with them to the new land. Each of these many cultures has made unique contributions to American life. Each group has added to the multicultural society that is America today.

Waves of Immigration

Many immigrant groups came to America in waves. In the early 1800s, economic conditions in Europe were growing harsh. Famine in Ireland led to a massive push of emigration of Irish men and women to the United States. A similar number of

German farmers and urban workers migrated to America. They were attracted by high wages, a growing number of jobs, and low land prices. Starting in 1880, huge numbers of people in southern and eastern Europe, including Italians, Russians, Poles, and Greeks, were facing rising populations and poor economies. To escape these conditions, they chose to immigrate to the United States. In the first 10 years of the 20th century, immigration from Europe was in the millions each year, with a peak of 8 million immigrants in 1910. In the 1930s, thousands of Jewish immigrants fled religious persecution in Nazi Germany and came to America.

Becoming a Legal Immigrant

There were few limits on the number of immigrants that could come to America until 1924. That year, Congress limited immigration to the United States to only 100,000 per year. In 1965, the number of immigrants allowed into the United States each year was raised from 100,000 to 290,000. In 1986, Congress further relaxed immigration rules, especially for immigrants from Cuba and Haiti. The new law allowed 1.5 million legal immigrants to enter the United States in 1990. Since then, more than half a million people have legally immigrated to the United States each year.

Not everyone who wants to immigrate to the United States is allowed to do so. The number of people from other countries who may immigrate to America is determined by a federal law called the Immigration and Naturalization Act (INA). This law was first passed in 1952. It has been amended (changed) many times since then.

Following the terrorist attacks on the World Trade Center in New York City and the Pentagon in Washington, D.C., in 2001, Congress made significant changes in the INA. One important change was to make the agency that administers laws concerning immigrants and other people entering the United States part of the Department of Homeland Security (DHS). The DHS is responsible for protecting the United States from attacks by terrorists. The new immigration agency is called the Citizenship and Immigration Service (CIS). It replaced the previous agency, which was called the Immigration and Naturalization Service (INS).

When noncitizens enter the United States, they must obtain official permission from the government to stay in the country. This permission is called a visa. Visas are issued by the CIS for a specific time period. In order to remain in the country permanently, an immigrant must obtain a permanent resident visa, also called a green card. This document allows a person to live, work, and study in the United States for an unlimited amount of time.

To qualify for a green card, an immigrant must have a sponsor. In most cases, a sponsor is a member of the immigrant's family who is a U.S. citizen or holds a green card. The government sets an annual limit of 226,000 on the number of family members who may be sponsored for permanent residence. In addition, no more than 25,650 immigrants may come from any one country.

In addition to family members, there are two other main avenues to obtaining a green card. A person may be sponsored by a U.S. employer or may enter the Green Card Lottery. An employer may sponsor a person who has unique work qualifications. The Green Card Lottery randomly selects 50,000 winners each year to receive green cards. Applicants for the lottery may be from any country from which immigration is allowed by U.S. law.

However, a green card does not grant an immigrant U.S. citizenship. Many immigrants have chosen to become citizens of the United States. Legal immigrants who have lived in the United States for at least five years and who meet other requirements may apply to become naturalized citizens. Once these immigrants qualify for citizenship, they become full-fledged citizens and have all the rights, privileges, and obligations of other U.S. citizens.

Even with these newer laws, there are always more people who want to immigrate to the United States than are allowed by law. As a result, some people choose to come to the United States illegally. Illegal immigrants do not have permission from the U.S. government to enter the country. Since 1980, the number of illegal immigrants entering the United States, especially from Central and South America, has increased greatly. These illegal immigrants are pushed by poverty in their homelands and pulled by the hope of a better life in the United States. Illegal immigration cannot be exactly measured, but it is believed that between 1 million and 3 million illegal immigrants enter the United States each year.

This series, Immigration to the United States, describes the history of the immigrant groups that have come to the United States. Some came because of the pull of America and the hope of a better life. Others were pushed out of their homelands. Still others were forced to immigrate as slaves. Whatever the reasons for their arrival, each group has a unique story and has made a unique contribution to the American way of life. 🟦

Right: Aztec merchants trade in the city of Tenochtitlán, the capital of the Aztec Empire before it was conquered by Spain.

Introduction

Mexican Immigration

The Journey North

For more than 150 years, Mexican immigrants have played an important role in the United States. After the Spanish conquest of Mexico in the 16th century, communities of Mexicans were established in Texas, New Mexico, Arizona, and California. These territories became part of the United States after the U.S.-Mexican War in the 1840s. The Mexicans who lived there suddenly became second-class U.S. citizens. Many Mexican landowners were stripped of their property, while others faced discrimination as they tried to claim land during the California gold rush. Gradually, these early immigrants were driven into low-paying jobs.

Nevertheless, large numbers of Mexican immigrants crossed the border into the United States during the late 19th and early 20th century. They were fleeing a crumbling economy and an unstable political situation in their homeland. They were also hoping to find greater economic opportunities in the United States. Some succeeded, but many others were not as successful. They usually lived in segregated Mexican-American communities, which meant that they were separated from other ethnic groups. Some chose to live among other Mexicans, but many had no other choice because they were not accepted in other areas. Many labored as poorly paid migrant farmworkers who moved from place to place to find work. Many Mexican immigrants were even targeted with racial violence.

Things began to improve as more Mexican immigrants crossed the border after World War II (1939–1945). In the 1960s Mexican Americans fought for their civil rights and promoted their culture, which helped them achieve equality under the law and greater acceptance by the majority in the United States. Nevertheless, some Mexican immigrants still faced serious problems. Still others were forced to hide from the law because they entered the United States illegally.

A huge wave of Mexican immigration started in the 1970s and continues today. It has made Mexicans the largest immigrant group entering the United States. As a result, the population of Mexican Americans has grown to more than 21 million. Despite the problems of illegal immigration, it is clear that these immigrants have enriched American society. Mexican Americans have become successful business owners, celebrated artists and writers, and strong leaders. They have also given the United States greater diversity in its language and customs and continue to become an increasingly important part of American culture in the 21st century. ❀

Opposite: *The Aztec king surrenders Mexico to the Spanish general Hernán Cortés in this painting by Miguel Gonzalez from 1698.*

Chapter One

Spanish Conquest and Early Immigration

Building an Empire

The Spanish Arrive

People have been moving northward from Mexico into what is now the United States for almost 500 years. The Spanish, who conquered Mexico, brought with them a language and traditions that have greatly influenced the United States, especially in the Southwest. The story of Mexican immigration begins with the arrival of Spanish explorers and soldiers near the Yucatán peninsula in the early 16th century.

In a letter to the Spanish king Charles I, written in 1520, Hernán Cortés described his entrance into the city of Tenochtitlán (modern-day Mexico City, in central Mexico):

This great city . . . is situated in this salt lake. . . . There are four avenues or entrances to the city, all of which are formed by artificial causeways, two spears' length in width.

Mexico

Cortés was a Spanish conquistador (conqueror) who had invaded the area now known as Mexico. Tenochtitlán was the capital of a great empire controlled by the Aztec that stretched over a large part of Mexico. The Aztec were the most powerful of many American Indian groups living in Mexico at this time. In about 1200, the powerful Aztec army had conquered other Indian tribes and forced them to pay taxes of gold, silver, copper, and food.

Cortés had landed on the eastern coast of Mexico in 1519 with about 500 soldiers. He was determined to conquer the Aztec and claim this territory in the New World, as the Europeans called North and South America, for Spain. He allied himself with other Indian tribes that had been defeated by the Aztec and hated them. Meanwhile, the Aztec emperor Montezuma did little to stop the Spaniards. Because Cortés seemed so powerful, Montezuma may have believed that he was the Aztec god Quetzalcoatl and could not be defeated. It was believed that no man was more powerful than a god.

Finally, Cortés reached Tenochtitlán, a city of more than 200,000 people. His letter to King Charles continues:

The city has many public squares, in which are situated the markets and other places for buying and selling. . . . Different kinds of cotton thread of all colors . . . are exposed for sale in one quarter of the market . . . deerskins dressed and undressed, dyed different colors; earthen-ware of a large size and excellent quality; large and small jars, jugs, pots, bricks, and endless variety of vessels, all made of fine clay, and all or most of them glazed and painted . . . as well as jewels of gold and silver.

It was the gold and silver that most interested Cortés and his men, who had heard stories about the fabulous riches of the Aztec. Although the Aztec outnumbered the Spaniards, Cortés managed to take Montezuma prisoner and forced him to order

*Hernán Cortés (left) stands with
Aztec emperor Montezuma.*

his subjects to collect as much gold and silver as they could from across the Aztec Empire. At first, the Aztec went along with this request and brought enormous amounts of treasure to Tenochtitlán. Soon, however, the Aztec revolted and drove the Spaniards out of the city. In return, the Spanish laid siege to Tenochtitlán and after three months defeated the Aztec.

Spaniards Take Control

The Spanish conquistadores took control of the Aztec Empire and all of Mexico, which became known as New Spain. They set up their capital, called Mexico City, on the site of Tenochtitlán. The Spanish residents of Mexico became the new aristocrats (wealthy landowners). The Indians were reduced to slavery, forced to work on the Spanish farms that were established across central Mexico. They were also required to dig for gold and silver in the nearby mines. Over several decades, some of the Spanish intermarried with the Aztec and other tribes, creating a new mixed race of settlers called mestizos. Mestizos had a much lower status in Mexico than the Spanish had. They did not have the same opportunities to acquire wealth and own large farms as the Spanish did. Instead, the mestizos became the working people of Mexico. They also looked for new opportunities northward and eventually began to emigrate to the present-day United States.

Explorers and Immigrants

M eanwhile, the Spanish began to explore the lands north of Mexico in what is now the United States. They had heard reports from Native Americans that more gold and silver might be found there. One of the earliest Spanish explorers to this area was Álvar Núñez Cabeza de Vaca, who traveled through present-day Texas, New Mexico, and Arizona in the 1530s. Back in Mexico, he told of hearing about the magnificent Seven Cities of Cíbola, which were supposed to be fabulously rich with treasures of gold.

To find out more about these cities, the Spanish sent out more expeditions. In 1540 an expedition under the command of Francisco Vásquez de Coronado headed northward and eventually reached the cities of Cíbola, in present-day Arizona. However, what Coronado found was not cities of gold, but Native American villages and farms. Finding no treasure, Coronado finally returned to Mexico City in 1542.

It's a Fact!

Álvar Núñez Cabeza de Vaca became famous among the Indians because he seemed capable of curing sick people with his prayers.

Although they found no golden cities, the Spanish did not leave empty-handed. Through their explorations, the Spanish claimed a large territory in what is now the southwestern United States. By the late 16th century, people from Mexico began to settle in this territory. This represented the first major movement of Mexican people northward into what is now the United States.

During the last years of the 16th century and the first years of the 17th century, more colonists began arriving in what is now New Mexico. Spanish priests known as missionaries soon trekked to the area with plans to convert the local Indians, or urge them to follow the Roman Catholic religion. Although the

Spanish missionaries soon converted an estimated 8,000 Native Americans, many of the Indians were converted by force. The Spaniards had superior weapons, and the Native Americans often had little choice but to do as the Spaniards told them.

The Spanish explorers searching for the Seven Cities of Cíbola may have expected to see grand cities like Tenochtitlán, built by the Aztec in Mexico.

In 1610, the Spanish established a new town that they named Santa Fe, which means "Holy Faith." By 1650, about 100 other towns were established in the territory, which the Spanish called the Kingdom and Provinces of New Mexico. Santa Fe became its capital.

The Spanish called their towns pueblos. The Spanish pueblos were eventually located in the present-day states of New Mexico, Arizona, Texas, Utah, Colorado, California, Kansas, and Nebraska. The influence of these early Mexican settlers and those who came after them can be found especially in those states that today border Mexico. Many U.S. towns in those states have Spanish names. Religious beliefs and local customs also show the influence of the Spanish settlers.

The Spanish brought practices that had a negative impact on the local Indian tribes. The Spanish set up the *encomienda* system, which they used in their other colonies. This system provided a piece of land to a settler and required that the local Indians pay the settler a yearly supply of corn from their own farms. This was a form of tribute, a payment that the Indians were forced to give the Spanish. In addition, the new settlers established the *repartimiento,* which required the Indians to work on the Spanish farms in return for pay. But many of the Indians were never paid and instead became more like slaves than regular workers for the Spanish rulers.

Meanwhile, Indians were also forced to work at the Catholic missions set up throughout the Southwest. They served the missionaries' meals and cleaned their living quarters, built the churches, and worked in the fields. Indians who refused to follow the missionaries' orders were brutally beaten. They were also forced to give up their ancient religious practices and convert to Christianity. These conditions led to resentment and often hatred between the Native Americans and the Mexican settlers. Sometimes the hatred boiled over into small rebellions.

Mexican Theater

Mexican theater during the 16th century and afterward showed the influence of both Indian and Spanish cultures. The Aztec held religious ceremonies called *miloles.* The Spanish portrayed Christian themes in their plays, called *pastores.* These two types of performances influenced the *mascaradas,* which were plays performed in Mexico and later in the southwestern United States when Spanish immigrants arrived there.

During the 1670s, however, tribal leaders met together to plan a much larger uprising. They sent messengers to Indian towns throughout the area with word that a rebellion was planned for August 11, 1680. Known as the Pueblo Rebellion, it took the Spanish settlers, who numbered about 2,800, almost completely by surprise. During the early days of the revolt, almost 400 settlers were killed.

The Indians remained in control of the area for more than a decade. In August 1692, the Spanish sent out a force to conquer the territory. The expedition recaptured Santa Fe and other Indian towns as well. In 1694, the Indians made a last stand, but they were defeated by the Spanish. Gradually, settlers came back to the area and began a process of resettlement that would continue over the next three centuries.

The First Missions

During the 18th and early 19th centuries, settlers from Mexico continued heading northward to other areas that are now part of the United States. These immigrants began to settle regions now known as Arizona, Texas, and California. Leading the new immigrants was a small group of Spanish soldiers and a dedicated band of Catholic priests, who established missions that can still be seen across the West today.

In his autobiography, a Catholic priest, Father Eusebio Kino, explained why he worked to establish missions among the Akimel O'odham (Pima) Indians in what is now southern Arizona:

> *With these new conversions [to Christianity] the Catholic dominion of the royal crown of our very catholic monarch Philip V, God preserve him, and our holy Roman Catholic Faith, will be extended. . . . Very extensive new lands, nations,*

rivers, seas, and people of this North America which hitherto have been unknown will be discovered and won; and, besides, thereby these Christian provinces will be more protected, safer, and more quiet.

Although many of the Indians converted to Catholicism, not all did so willingly, and they were generally not happy with the Spanish settlement. The missions that Father Kino established were attacked by Apache Indians. Other Spanish missions were also raided by the Apache and other tribes beginning in 1751.

The mission church of San Jose de la Laguna, built between 1699 and 1701 near present-day Albuquerque, New Mexico, is a well-preserved example of the Catholic missions built by the Spanish throughout the West.

Texas and California

Meanwhile, Spanish priests and soldiers were leading expeditions to what is now Texas. In 1718 the Spanish built a mission and presidio, or fort, at San Antonio. In this area, the Comanche Indians raided the Spanish settlements. As a result, the number of new settlers in Texas remained small, reaching only about 3,500 by the beginning of the 19th century.

New settlements were also being established in California. Father Junípero Serra, a Catholic priest, led an expedition that reached San Diego on July 1, 1769, and built a presidio and a mission there. Father Serra established nine more missions in California over the next two decades.

After Father Serra's death in 1784, missions were built along a road called El Camino Real ("the Royal Highway"), which stretched for about 500 miles (800 km) from San Diego to San Francisco. The missions raised herds of cattle and sheep, grew grain, and cultivated lush vineyards that produced large grape harvests. Local Indians did most of the work, after being taught by the monks how to raise crops and domestic animals unfamiliar to them. However, the Indians were treated like slaves by the missionaries and often beaten if they did not do their work. As many as 100,000 of them died from overwork and diseases.

An overland route from central Mexico to the San Gabriel Mission near present-day Los Angeles, California, was established in 1774. Along with El Camino Real, this route brought supplies to the settlers and helped create other new settlements in California. In 1781, however, an Indian uprising closed the route. Over the next two decades, few settlers came to California.

Opposite: *The Santa Fe Trail, shown here in the 1840s, was the major trade route between New Mexico and Missouri.*

Chapter Two

Mexico and the United States

Immigrants in the Southwest

Relations with the United States

During the early 19th century, trading ships from the United States arrived in California. One of these ships was the *Lelia Byrd*. Its captain was William Shaler. In 1808, Shaler published a journal about his trips to California. He was unfairly critical of the Spanish immigrants there. He said that they were "indolent" (lazy) and "fond of spirituous liquors" (drinking alcohol). Shaler also noted that the population was small, only about 3,000, and that the "conquest of this country would be absolutely nothing; it would fall without an effort to the most inconsiderable force." In his opinion, California could easily be conquered.

While Shaler was making his observations of California, settlers from the United States were moving west. In 1803, President Thomas Jefferson had purchased the Louisiana Territory from France for $15 million. The addition of the Louisiana Territory almost doubled the size of the United States. It included part or all of 13 current states, including Louisiana, Arkansas, Missouri, Oklahoma, Nebraska, Iowa, and South Dakota.

It's a Fact!

Between 1830 and 1848, traders used the Old Spanish Trail that ran from Santa Fe to Los Angeles. Traders carried woolen items from Santa Fe to California, where they bartered (traded) them for mules and horses to bring back to Santa Fe. The Old Spanish Trail was originally developed by Native Americans to connect their villages.

Settlers from the United States began moving into the Louisiana Territory and also into nearby Texas. Much of the soil in eastern Texas was fertile and excellent for growing cotton. The land was also cheap, only 10 cents an acre compared with $1.25 per acre in the United States. This meant that settlers could establish large, productive farms in the area. The Spanish government welcomed settlers from the United States.

Meanwhile, New Mexico continued to develop as a Spanish colony. The settlers there raised herds of cows, horses, and sheep. They used the sheep's wool to make blankets, cloth, and stockings. To supply some of the other needs of the settlers, a brisk trade developed between the United States and New Mexico. As traders from Missouri traveled back and forth from New Mexico, a new trade route was established. It became known as the Santa Fe Trail.

The Mexican Revolution

While conditions along the frontier were slowly changing with the arrival of more and more settlers, a major upheaval occurred inside New Spain. Beginning in 1811, a revolution swept the government, which led to Mexico breaking away from Spain. The revolution was begun by Miguel Hidalgo y Costilla, a Catholic priest. Born in 1753, Hidalgo was a member of the Creole class in Mexico. (Creoles, as the term was used in Mexico, were people born in Mexico to Spanish parents.) Settlers who had been born in Spain looked down on the Creoles and prevented

Miguel Hidalgo y Costilla led the fight for Mexican independence from Spain.

them from filling most of the highest offices in the government of New Spain. Hidalgo joined with other Creoles to discuss ways to increase their power in Mexico.

In 1810, Hidalgo and his group decided that the time had come to begin a revolution to free Mexico from Spanish rule. Gathering a large army, Hidalgo was successful in taking control of many towns. However, in 1811, Hidalgo was captured by the Spanish army, put on trial, and executed. Even so, the rebels eventually succeeded in driving Spain from Mexico, and in 1823 Mexico became a democratic republic, much like the United States.

On the Frontier

The upheaval in Mexico had an enormous impact on the frontier. Soldiers had to leave the presidios to fight in the civil war in Mexico. This left the frontier settlements open to more raids by the Apache and the Comanche. In California, the settlers decided to take control of the lands that belonged to the Catholic missions, mostly because the Catholic Church had supported the Spanish government during the revolution. During the 1830s and 1840s, all of the mission lands were taken over by well-to-do ranchers in California. The Indians, who had worked the mission lands for decades, received nothing.

On these large ranches, the Mexicans of California, who called themselves Californios, raised citrus fruits—such as oranges and lemons—and corn, wheat, and cattle. The cattle supplied not only beef but also hides, which were used to make shoes and clothing, and tallow, their dried fat, which was turned into soap and candles. Ships from Boston, Massachusetts, and other New England ports traveled to California to trade with the ranchers. In return, they sold the Californios jewelry, furniture, coffee, tea, sugar, spices, silk clothing, and other goods.

War with Mexico

Meanwhile, settlers from the United States continued to head westward, establishing new settlements in California and Texas. Tensions began to build between the American settlers in Texas, who far outnumbered the Mexican residents, and the government in Mexico City. One reason was that the American immigrants often acted like an independent community within Mexico. They traded with the United States and looked north for support instead of to the Mexican government. The tension finally erupted into the Texas Revolution in 1835, when Texans fought for their independence from Mexico.

In an effort to stamp out the independence movement, the Mexican president, General Antonio López de Santa Anna, marched north to San Antonio with a large army of more than 6,000 troops. In February 1836, he took up a position outside the Alamo, an old Spanish mission that had been occupied by Texans. Santa Anna's army far outnumbered the small band of Texans, and after a siege of almost two weeks, the Mexicans stormed the Alamo on March 6, killing all the defenders.

"Remember the Alamo" became a war cry among Texans fighting for their freedom. A few weeks later, the Texans had their revenge. Texas troops commanded by General Samuel Houston surprised Santa Anna's army at the Battle of San Jacinto, capturing the Mexican leader. To gain his freedom, Santa Anna agreed to recognize that Texas was independent of Mexico.

Texas remained independent until 1845, when it became part of the United States. By then, American president James K. Polk had decided that the time had come for the United States to take control of the rest of the Mexican empire in the West.

In 1846 battles broke out along the Rio Grande ("Big River") between U.S. troops led by General Zachary Taylor and the

Mexican army. As a result, the United States declared war on Mexico. Taylor's forces defeated the Mexican army and pushed southward into Mexico. Meanwhile, Polk sent an army westward and eventually captured New Mexico, Arizona, and California.

The U.S. forces invading Mexico captured Mexico City in September 1847. This brought an end to the war. By the Treaty of Guadalupe Hidalgo, signed early the following year, Mexico agreed to give more than half of its territory to the United States. The war settled the boundary line of Texas at the Rio Grande, while the New Mexico territory and California also became part of the United States.

Suddenly, about 80,000 Mexicans living in California, New Mexico, Arizona, and Texas had become U.S. citizens.

California

About the same time that the U.S.-Mexican War ended, gold was discovered in California. In 1849, thousands of people went to California, hoping to get rich by mining gold. Among them were 25,000 immigrants from northern Mexico, who had worked in the gold and silver mines located there. When they reached California, however, the Mexicans were not welcomed by the other miners. This pattern was repeated over and over again for Mexican immigrants throughout the last half of the 19th century.

The Mexican miners who arrived in California immediately discovered that they were not accepted as equals by the Anglos, that is, the white people who came from the United States. The Mexicans were treated badly because many of the Anglos, who had no experience in mining, feared that the immigrants would be more successful in finding gold. According to historian Manuel Gonzales, there was also a great deal of racism involved in the Anglos' treatment of the Mexicans. Most of the Mexicans were mestizos, descendants of the Spanish and Native Americans of Mexico. The whites looked down on them because of their brown skin. The whites called the Mexicans "greasers" because of their silky black hair.

Not only did Mexican immigrants face discrimination in California, but many of the Californios faced the same type of treatment at the hands of the Anglos. Over time, many well-to-do Californios lost their wealth and were forced to take low-paying jobs working for Anglo landowners. Some became vaqueros, or cowboys, tending the large herds of cattle that were raised on the huge Anglo estates. The poorer Mexicans, who had once worked for the Californios, also found themselves working for Anglo estate owners. These Mexican workers, called peons, received low wages for long hours of work on farms and cattle ranches.

Arizona

When Arizona became part of the United States, its population was very small, between 1,000 and 1,500 people. Few Anglos came to the area at first. Arizona was a place where people stopped only briefly on their way to the California gold fields. By 1860, Tucson, the main community in Arizona, had a population of only 925 people. Only about 170 were Anglos. In Tucson and other parts of Arizona, Anglos intermarried with the Mexican population.

Celebrations in the Mexican Community

During the 19th century, Mexican communities carried on a rich cultural life. The Catholic Church was an important center of each village. The bells in village churches were frequently rung to announce important events such as church services, marriage ceremonies, or funerals. *Violinistas* (violin players) or other musicians led wedding processions from the church and also played at fiestas, or parties. The fiesta might include a church service, a craft fair, a large meal, and a dance. Fiestas are still popular celebrations in the Mexican-American community. At Christmas (Navidad) and other holiday fiestas, Mexican-American children, as they still do today, danced under a piñata, a decorated container filled with candies and toys, suspended from above. They hit the piñata with sticks until it broke and spilled its goodies onto the floor.

Mexican Americans enjoy a traditional type of music known as mariachi. Mariachi grew out of American Indian music in Mexico played with rattles, drums, and horns, as well as Spanish music played with violins and guitars. A mariachi band now includes as many as eight violins, two trumpets, and a guitar.

Gradually, Mexican immigrants began arriving in Arizona. They came for several reasons. Some were looking for better jobs. Wages in Mexico were extremely low. The wages paid to peons remained the same throughout most of the 19th century, while the price of some food, such as corn, doubled. The peons' wages could not keep up with these price increases. Meanwhile, in Arizona, new silver and gold mines were opening up that offered jobs to Mexican immigrants.

In the 1870s, the Southern Pacific Railroad was built in Arizona and among its passengers were many Anglos who wanted jobs in the mining industry. As the Anglo population increased in Arizona, relations with the Mexicans grew worse. The situation was similar to that in California, where Anglo miners felt threatened by the Mexicans. Some Mexican miners were murdered, and others, suspected of crimes, were executed without a trial by Anglo mobs. In 1872, Don Francisco Gandara, who was accused of killing a white man, was gunned down by Anglos in front of his family at home.

A Mexican-American cowboy, called a vaquero, herds cattle in Arizona in the mid-1800s.

Many Mexicans tried to protect themselves against the Anglos by withdrawing into their own communities. Mexicans began to show pride in their own heritage and referred to themselves as La Raza. This is a term that means "the Mexican people" or "race." Mexicans often grouped together in certain areas of towns, known as barrios, or in rural villages, known as *ranchos*. The Mexican community also began to form mutual aid societies, called *mutualistas*, which offered help to Mexican families and preserved Mexican culture. As one historian explained, "Mutual aid societies met the material needs of their members with emergency loans and other forms of financial assistance. They also . . . sponsored other institutions like newspapers and private schools."

New Mexico

To the east in New Mexico, life for Mexican immigrants was different than in Arizona. When it became part of the United States, New Mexico had a population of more than

70,000 people. It had been the most heavily populated area of the Mexican empire. At first, the few Anglos who came to New Mexico intermarried with the local families. But unlike in California and Arizona, where Mexicans were soon overwhelmed by the Anglo population, the population of New Mexico remained mostly Mexican. This helped new Mexican immigrants fit easily into a familiar culture. Albuquerque and Santa Fe were important communities in New Mexico. Railroads took cattle raised in New Mexico to communities throughout the United States, where they were slaughtered for food. In addition, rich Mexican landowners known as *ricos* maintained huge herds of sheep. According to one estimate, there were 4 million sheep in New Mexico in 1880.

A Visitor to New Mexico

In 1857 an Anglo visitor to New Mexico, William Watts, described some of his experiences in a new culture. He explained that many of the houses were built of adobe. This was dirt mixed with water and dried to form building blocks. The blocks were held together by mud mixed with straw. A thin covering of this mud was applied to the outside of the house to help it withstand wind and rain.

The front doors of a Mexican home opened onto a patio, which was connected to the *sala*, the main room of the house. The floors were covered with woolen rugs, and the dark walls were lined with colorful cloth. The Mexicans,

Watts continued, had little furniture. "Few chairs or wooden seats of any kind are used, but in their stead mattresses are folded up and placed around the room, next to the wall, which being covered with blankets, make a pleasant seat and serve the place of sofas. . . . At night they are unrolled and spread out for beds."

Watts also commented on the foods that were eaten in Mexico. These included tortillas, thin breads made out of corn or flour, which were often eaten with frijoles, or beans. Another Mexican dish was chili con carne. This was a mixture of beef and tomatoes, spiced with hot chili peppers.

Much of the work on the sheep farms was done by *pobres*, the poor Mexicans. The enormous herds of sheep were maintained by shepherds, some of whom were immigrants from Mexico. During the evenings, for entertainment, some of the shepherds would compose ballads, or *corridos*. According to one observer, "The sheepherder watched his flock by day, traveling many miles while the sheep grazed on the range. As his flock pastured, he sat on a rock or on his coat; he whittled some object or composed songs or poetry until it was time to move the flock to water or better pasture."

Texas

The large herds of sheep that grazed over many miles of New Mexico regularly brought shepherds into conflict with cattle ranchers from west Texas. These ranchers wanted the range as pasture for their cows. Range wars broke out during the 1870s and 1880s, often sparked by racial tensions between Anglo cattle ranchers and Mexican sheep owners.

In south Texas, however, there was a large population of Mexicans who had moved there before the U.S.-Mexican War. In addition, more immigrants were regularly crossing the Rio Grande from Mexico. This large Mexican population battled against the prejudice it encountered from the Anglos.

Among the most famous leaders of this resistance was Juan Cortina. Born in northern Mexico in 1824, Cortina lived on a large cattle ranch owned by his family. During the 1850s, Cortina moved to Texas to manage some of his family's estates and become a rancher. On July 13, 1859, in Brownsville, Texas, Cortina saw an Anglo law-enforcement official beating up a Mexican. When the official refused to stop, Cortina shot him and took the Mexican to safety. In the fall, he returned to

Brownsville with a large group of men and executed several Anglos who had killed Mexicans. Cortina then established the Republic of the Rio Grande. "Mexicans!" he announced. "My part is taken . . . to me is entrusted the work of breaking the chains of your slavery. . . . The Lord will enable me, with powerful arm, to fight against our enemies."

Eventually, Cortina left Brownsville, but he was chased by American authorities who wanted to capture him. However, many Mexicans living in Texas, known as Tejanos, supported him. Cortina was able to escape across the border to Mexico, where he was finally captured by Mexican authorities and imprisoned in 1876. He spent the next 14 years behind bars and died soon afterward.

While the Mexicans sought to maintain their culture in Texas, the railroads brought more and more Anglos to the area. In Texas, as in much of the West, Mexican immigrants found themselves treated as second-class citizens. By the beginning of the 20th century, some communities in Texas practiced segregation in their schools. That is, there were different schools for Mexican-American and Anglo children. Anglos kept most new immigrants, as well as Mexican Americans who had been born in the West, out of high-paying jobs. In addition, only Anglos became important political officeholders, such as state governors and members of the U.S. Congress, in the West. ▨

Opposite: *This Mexican-American home in Santa Fe, New Mexico, in the 1800s, is made of adobe.*

Chapter Three

New Immigration Begins

1900–1930

A Large Migration

O ver three decades, beginning in 1900, an estimated
1.5 million Mexicans left their homeland and emigrated
to the United States. According to historians, this large
migration was powered by many different forces. Events inside
Mexico persuaded, or pushed, many Mexicans to leave home
and head northward. In addition, opportunities in the United
States pulled Mexicans from their homeland, drawing them into
a new country.

This document is part of an application for an American passport by a
young Mexican American who was reentering the United States at
Angel Island, California, in 1919.

Conditions in Mexico

During his 30-year term as president of Mexico, from the 1880s to 1910, Porfirio Díaz changed the country. President Díaz improved the Mexican economy by encouraging investment from the United States in a variety of projects. Among these projects were the Mexican railroads. During the Díaz presidency, almost 15,000 miles (24,000 km) of railroads were built. These railroads connected the various regions of Mexico, while also linking them to cities in the southwestern United States. The vast railroad network also aided in the development of mines in Mexico. Large deposits of copper, silver, gold, and lead were taken from mines located across Mexico and shipped out along the new rail lines. Meanwhile, U.S. and British companies dug wells to take advantage of Mexico's large oil reserves. As more and more people arrived in Mexico, new industries sprang up in cities such as Monterrey, near the Texas border, and Veracruz, along the coast.

Foreigners were not the only ones to benefit from the growth of the Mexican economy. New laws enabled Mexican landowners to buy up more property. Much of this property was owned by Indians who had farmed it for hundreds of years, since before the arrival of the Spaniards. The landowners paid low, unfair prices for the valuable land. The Indians had little choice but to accept the prices.

While the Indians lost their land, the rich property owners sold some of the land to the railroads and became even wealthier. Others invested in mining companies, sugar mills, and other businesses. Don Luis Terrazas, for example, owned steel mills, coal mines, and telephone companies. He was also one of the wealthiest hacienda, or ranch, owners in Mexico, with approximately 3 million acres (1.2 million ha) of land.

*Porfirio Díaz was the president
of Mexico for 30 years.*

While some people grew rich under President Díaz, he did not benefit the poor of Mexico. Although some of them found employment in the mines and factories, the wages were lower than they could have earned for similar jobs in the United States. Most poor Mexicans were peons living on the large haciendas, where they worked long hours seven days a week. They tended sheep, herded cattle, and grew crops for the *patrón,* or wealthy landowner. In return, they received a small house for their families as well as a small plot of land where they could grow their own vegetables. According to historians Michael Meyer and William Sherman, the homes were

> *. . . miserable, one-room, floorless, windowless adobe shacks. Water had to be carried in daily, often from long distances. . . . Twice a day [on short breaks from work] a few minutes would be set aside to consume tortillas wrapped around beans and chili, washed down with a few gulps of black coffee. . . . Protein in the form of meat, fish, or fowl, even on the cattle haciendas, was a luxury. . . . Infant mortality [death rates] on many haciendas exceeded 25 percent.*

These high death rates resulted largely from a poor diet, unclean living conditions without proper toilets or clean water, and no medical care.

Most peons were too poor to afford any better. They were forced to buy what they needed at the store owned by the *patrón* and pay whatever prices he charged. If a peon complained about the prices or his low wages, he might be punished by the *mayor domo,* the manager of the estate. As a result, most peons were in constant debt to the *patrón,* unable to afford what they needed at the store and always forced to borrow more money. Furthermore, the law prevented peons from leaving their hacienda and looking for a better job elsewhere in Mexico. Many found that they had no choice but to leave Mexico for the United States.

Revolt in Mexico

For some political leaders in Mexico, the advances made by the Díaz regime did not seem worth the price being paid by hundreds of thousands of peons. Among those who spoke out against Díaz were three brothers named Jesus, Ricardo, and Enrique Magón. In 1900, the Magóns started a newspaper, Regeneración, which printed articles criticizing Díaz's government. The Magóns were soon jailed by the government, which did not permit free speech. After being released, they started another newspaper and once again found themselves under arrest. After being freed from prison the second time, the Magóns left Mexico and went to the United States. They settled in San Antonio, Texas, where they reopened Regeneración, continuing their verbal attacks on the Mexican government.

From the United States, the Magóns also started rebellions in an effort to overthrow the Díaz government. As one editorial in their newspaper stated, "Forever—for as long as Mexico can remember—today's slavery will be identified with the name of the devil that made it all possible. His name is Porfirio Díaz." When Díaz tried to have one of the Magón brothers assassinated, they moved their newspaper out of San Antonio northward to St. Louis, Missouri.

*Pancho Villa (left), a Mexican rebel leader, is pictured
with part of his small army in 1914. Although the legendary Villa,
who was born Doroteo Arango, was an outlaw, some
Mexicans considered him a hero.*

Meanwhile, inside Mexico itself, the movement against Díaz was gathering strength. Strikes broke out among Mexican workers at mines and factories and were brutally put down by government soldiers. Among those who spoke out against Díaz was Francisco Madero. Madero, the son of a wealthy hacienda owner, recognized the plight of the peons on his family's property and tried to improve it. Eventually, he entered politics and challenged Díaz in the presidential election of 1910. Díaz jailed Madero to force him out of the election race. After his release from prison, Madero left the country for the United States. From San Antonio, he issued a call to Mexicans to rise up and overthrow the Díaz regime. Rebel armies were formed across Mexico that eventually overthrew the Díaz government, forcing the dictator to leave Mexico in 1911.

The overthrow of Díaz did not mark the end of political turmoil in Mexico but only the beginning. After becoming president to replace Díaz, Francisco Madero could not satisfy all the rebel leaders who had helped put him in power. One of these leaders, Emiliano Zapata, called on the government to immediately turn over lands from the rich to help the poor. When Madero did not act, Zapata began a revolt, which was joined by other rebel armies. Madero was overthrown and murdered in 1913. Over the next several years, other politicians seized power and were later overthrown. Mexico was torn apart by civil war that involved rebel leaders like Zapata and Pancho Villa.

The civil war in Mexico had a terrible effect on the lives of peasants throughout the country. As rebel armies marched across the landscape, they destroyed crops, stole food from the peons, and destroyed their homes. According to one estimate, 1.5 to 2 million people were killed during the civil war. Some were randomly murdered by rebel soldiers, while others were forced to join the rebel armies and died in battle.

Immigrants to the United States

The violence terrified many Mexicans. To escape the civil war, thousands of immigrants fled from Mexico and journeyed to safety in El Norte, the north. In October 1913, an estimated 8,000 Mexicans left their homeland and reached Eagle Pass, Texas, on a single day. Most of the new immigrants left

Mexico for what they expected to be a temporary stay in the United States. They hoped to earn some money and return home again, after the violence of the civil war had ended.

As they crossed the border, the Mexicans came up against the immigration laws that affected everyone entering the United States. Mexicans were supposed to pay eight dollars to cross the border and then prove that they could read English. However, U.S. officials frequently overlooked these laws because of the enormous demand for workers for farms, mines, and railroads in the Southwest.

The majority of Mexican immigrants remained in the southwestern United States because it was near their homes in Mexico. In addition, Mexican-American communities had already sprung up in this area, and the new immigrants felt comfortable among other people like themselves. Jobs for farmworkers were plentiful in the cotton fields of Texas, where thousands of Mexican immigrants put in long hours each day. Entire families worked together planting cottonseeds, tending the small cotton plants, and weeding the soil. Often they used *el cortito*, a short hoe, which forced the farm laborers to bend over to do their work. After endless hours and days bending over cotton plants, many farmworkers developed severe back problems.

After a cotton crop was picked, these Mexican laborers and their families, called migrant workers, would move on from the cotton farms to find other work. Many went to farms farther north

It's a Fact!

Many Mexicans entered the United States with visas, that is, permission to be residents but not citizens. However, an unknown number crossed the border illegally without visas. In 1924, the U.S. Border Patrol began policing the border with Mexico. But there were not enough border guards to stop all the illegal immigrants entering the United States. Professional smugglers, called coyotes, helped the Mexicans cross the border illegally.

in California, Colorado, and Utah. In these states, they found jobs harvesting sugar beets, the raw ingredient for sugar, and picking other vegetables. Some of the immigrants found employment in the mines throughout the Southwest. With a long history of experience as miners in Mexico, the new immigrants easily obtained jobs in the copper, gold, and silver mines that were being developed in the United States. Others went to work on the railroads. Tracks had already been laid between the U.S. Southwest and Mexico during the last part of the 19th century. However, the railroad tracks needed constant maintenance and repair. These jobs were readily available to the Mexican immigrants.

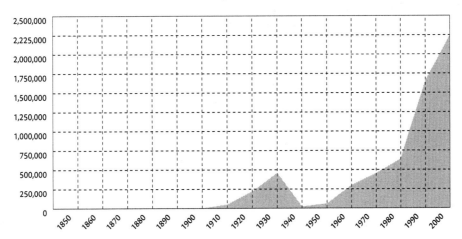

Mexican Immigration to America

Immigrant Lifestyles

What the Mexican immigrants encountered in the United States often seemed little better than what they had left behind. Instead of the *mayor domos,* the immigrants had to deal with the *contratistas,* or labor contractors. These were generally other Mexican Americans who gathered a group of immigrants to work for an employer on a large farm or in some other business. Most *contratistas* paid their workers as little as possible. Laborers tried to resist by picking fewer crops or intentionally breaking farm tools to slow the work. However, there was little else they could do to fight back.

The farmworkers, known as campesinos, often set up camps near their jobs, where they lived in tents, rundown shacks, and even barns that were no different from the houses they had left in Mexico. City workers increasingly began to establish more permanent homes in barrios located in major cities. These "little Mexicos," as they were called, grew up in cities such as Denver, Colorado; Chicago, Illinois; and Detroit, Michigan. In Detroit, for example, Mexicans who had come north on the railroads worked in the automobile industry. Other barrios that had already been established, such as those in Los Angeles and San Antonio, expanded as more immigrants arrived from Mexico.

Women in the Workplace

Mexico had a long tradition of keeping women out of the workplace so they could perform what were considered their primary responsibilities of caring for a home and raising children. However, Mexican men's low wages forced many Mexicans to recognize that women had to work outside the home to support their families. In major cities, more and more Mexican-American women obtained jobs in factories during the 1920s. Many others worked side by side with their husbands in the fields, hoeing and harvesting.

Mexican immigrants to the United States brought their culture and traditions with them. This group performs a traditional Aztec dance at a fiesta.

In these barrios, Mexican Americans established new businesses, such as restaurants, grocery stores, and cantinas, or taverns. They went to movie theaters that featured the latest productions from Hollywood and put on fiestas to celebrate Mexican holidays. Many of the residents in the barrios were peons who had come from Mexico looking for jobs in the cities.

In addition to the peons, some middle-class Mexicans had also fled the political turmoil in their country. They included doctors and lawyers, who opened offices in the barrios. Most Mexican Americans lived in their own ethnic communities. The primary reason for this was the prejudice they encountered from Anglos. As historians Richard Griswold Del Castillo and Arnoldo De Leon wrote, "Anglos kept Mexicans from [public] swimming pools, movie houses, barber shops, and eating places and openly displayed signs that read 'No Mexicans Allowed' or 'No Mexicans Wanted.'"

Like many other Mexican immigrants during the first decades of the 20th century, these two laborers found work on the Pennsylvania Railroad.

Mexican immigrants who worked on the railroad were paid less than white workers for the same jobs and forced to live in separate quarters. For many white Americans, the Mexican stereotype was Pancho Villa, who rode around the countryside and shot up villages. Magazines and movies reinforced this image of Mexicans, increasing the Anglo prejudice against them. Mexican Americans tried to deal with these problems with the help of the *mutualistas*. In addition, some workers joined labor unions (organizations that fought for workers' rights) and went on strike for better wages. Strikes occurred along the railroads in Arizona and in California. However, white railroad workers generally refused to help the Mexican strikers, and the strikes failed. Strikes also broke out on the large fruit and vegetable farms in southern California, where Mexican workers demanded higher wages. These strikes were more successful, but the living and working conditions for most Mexican Americans changed little as a result of these efforts.

Opposite: *Mexican farmworkers, pictured in 1942, wave American and Mexican flags. Millions of Mexican workers flocked to the United States during World War II to fill jobs that had been left by men going to war.*

Chapter Four

Immigrants Depart and Return

*The Great Depression
and World War II*

Hard Times

In 1930, the United States was plunged into the worst economic slump in its history, the Great Depression. Just over a decade later, America entered World War II in 1941. Both events had a profound impact on the lives of Mexican-American immigrants.

The level of unemployment during the worst years of the Great Depression in the early 1930s is almost unimaginable today. In 1929, before the depression began, only 1.5 million people were out of work, or about 3 percent of the workforce. By 1933, approximately 25 percent of America's workforce, more than 12 million people, were unemployed. Factories closed, retail businesses went bankrupt, banks failed, and families lost their homes and farms by the thousands. The flow of Mexican immigrants into the United States suddenly came to a halt. The United States was no longer a land of opportunity. For many of the Mexicans already living in the United States, the depression signaled an end to their hopes for better lives.

Not only did these immigrants have to cope with unemployment, they also faced increased resentment from their Anglo neighbors. Anglos asked themselves why their country should have to look out for these unemployed foreigners.

Many Anglos believed that charity should not be given to the Mexican Americans. Many Mexican Americans were competing with Anglos for the few jobs that were still available during the depression. Describing the situation in California, historian Carey McWilliams wrote, "When it became apparent . . . that the program for the relief of the unemployed would assume huge proportions in the Mexican quarter, the community swung to a determination to oust [throw out] the Mexicans."

Meanwhile, Mexican Americans who found themselves out of work decided that they might be better off returning to relatives who lived across the border in Mexico. Beginning in 1931, thousands of Mexican Americans began trekking back to Mexico. They were often assisted by charitable organizations and *mutualistas* as well as Mexican consuls, or diplomats who represented Mexico in many large American cities. Approximately 400,000 Mexican Americans went to Mexico in this massive reverse migration. While most went voluntarily, others were rounded up and forced to go. Some of them were the American-born children of Mexicans. Since they had been born in the United States, these young people were legally U.S. citizens and had every right to remain in the country.

A migrant Mexican worker poses with his baby near their home in California during the Great Depression.

Competing for Jobs

While some immigrants returned to Mexico, thousands more remained in the United States. Many were forced to compete for a reduced number of jobs, especially in farming.

During the depression, a massive drought struck the Midwest. Weeks of no rain turned vast farmlands into a giant dust bowl. As small Anglo farmers saw their land literally blow away, they packed up their belongings and headed west. Some went to Texas and Arizona, while others settled in the fertile valleys of California. Thousands of unemployed workers were willing to take any kind of job, even the low-paying work of picking fruits and vegetables in the fields. In the past, these jobs had belonged primarily to Mexican immigrants working as migrant laborers. Now, these immigrants were pushed out of work by the new families arriving in California. The Anglos also took jobs in the canneries, where fruits and vegetables were canned for shipment to other parts of the country.

✳✳✳ Women in Charge

Among the leaders of the unions were several Mexican-American women. One of them was Josefina Fierro de Bright. Born in Mexico in 1920, Josefina Fierro de Bright traveled to California with her family, who worked as campesinos. She attended college at the University of California at Los Angeles (UCLA), but she left to join the labor movement. De Bright also became an active member of the Spanish-Speaking Congress. Formed in 1938, this organization was dedicated to achieving equality and ending discrimination against Mexican and other Hispanic immigrants.

Some Mexican Americans fought back. They continued to join unions and stage strikes to save their jobs and improve their working conditions. During the 1930s, the major labor unions in the United States did not represent unskilled workers. Most of the unions, such as the American Federation of Labor (AFL), represented craftsmen such as carpenters. Therefore, the unskilled Mexican Americans formed their own union, called the Confederation of Mexican Farmworkers' and Workers' Unions. This union grew out of a *mutualista*. Mexican Americans also joined other unions, such as the United Cannery, Agricultural, Packing, and Allied Workers of America.

However, most Mexican Americans never joined the unions. They could not afford to pay the union dues that were used to support strikes and pay for organizing efforts. In addition, many Mexican workers had come into the United States illegally. They did not want to do anything, such as participate in a strike, that would bring them to the attention of the authorities. As a result, the Mexican-American labor union movement made little progress during the 1930s.

The New Deal and World War II

In 1932, Americans elected Franklin D. Roosevelt as president of the United States. Roosevelt offered the American people a program called the New Deal. It included public works projects, such as building roads and bridges, that were paid for by the federal government. These programs provided jobs for hundreds of thousands of Americans, including Mexican Americans. The many Mexican Americans who had crossed the border illegally, however, did not benefit from these programs because they did not have visas or were not U.S. citizens. While the government programs helped people survive the worst years of the depression, an improving economy gradually began providing more jobs for people by the late 1930s.

However, it was the outbreak of World War II in Europe in 1939 that revived the American economy. On December 7, 1941, Japanese planes attacked the American naval base at Pearl Harbor, Hawaii. The next day, the United States entered World War II, joining the Allies against Japan and Germany. America's factories went into high gear producing weapons, uniforms, food, and other supplies that were essential for the war effort.

As the United States went to war, hundreds of thousands of men went into the armed forces, leaving many job openings in farming and in factories. Mexican immigrants began streaming into the United States once again to fill these positions. In 1942, President Roosevelt signed an agreement with Mexican president Manuel Ávila Camacho to establish the Bracero Program. (*Bracero* is another word for laborer.) Under this program, recruiting stations were set up in Mexico to gather immigrants to work on large farms in the United States. The program lasted for 22 years and included almost 5 million Mexican immigrants. They lived in the United States for short periods, three to six months, while they harvested fruits and vegetables. Living conditions for braceros were frequently just as bad as they had been for the campesinos in the past. Even so, the program provided jobs for many immigrants, who took the money they earned back home to Mexico to help support their families.

In addition to working on farms, Mexican immigrants migrated to large cities to take over factory jobs. Barrios in San Antonio and Los Angeles expanded as more immigrants entered them from the South. In San Antonio, the barrio presented a mixed picture, according to one observer:

Unpainted shacks . . . rest on stilts and lean precariously in all directions; dogs bark, children yell, and radios blare in every hovel. But the windows are decorated with plants, feeble shrubs sprout in the dirt yards and morning-glories [tall flowers] climb the fence posts. Every corner has its grocery store and beer hall.

As more Mexican immigrants arrived in the United States, racial tensions increased, especially in Los Angeles. After the Japanese attack on Pearl Harbor, the West Coast of the United States braced for a possible invasion from Japan. Although a Japanese invasion never occurred, Anglos were very suspicious of the Japanese Americans living in the West. As a result, 100,000 Japanese Americans were rounded up and taken to camps, where they had to stay for the rest of the war.

These negative attitudes about Japanese Americans affected other immigrant groups, including Mexicans. Many Anglos had long considered Mexicans to be second-class citizens. Increasing numbers of immigrants took over jobs that had been held by Anglos who were going off to war. Eventually, violence between rival groups of young Mexican Americans boiled over into violence between Mexican Americans and Anglos.

Mexican Americans in World War II

Historians believe that 250,000 to 500,000 Mexican Americans fought in World War II. Twelve of these men won the highest award given by the United States to soldiers, the Congressional Medal of Honor. Among these Medal of Honor winners was Sergeant Jose M. Lopez from Texas. When the Allied forces invaded Europe in 1944, Lopez participated in the advance that finally defeated Nazi Germany. During one battle, he killed over 100 Nazi soldiers.

Some Mexican-American women also served in the armed forces. Many others took factory jobs that had been left open when men joined the military.

The Zoot-Suiters

In 1942, a popular style of clothing among many young Mexican-American men was the zoot suit. The zoot suit represented a whole way of life, symbolizing the resentment felt by many Mexican-American youth against the attitudes of Anglos, who looked down on them. At dances and parties, these young men, also called pachucos (possibly after a city in Mexico), wore baggy pants and oversized coats (known as zoot suits), while the Mexican-American women dressed in short skirts. These fashions made them stand out from other young people. Boys combed their hair in a style called the ducktail, which looked from the back like the tail of a duck. Some had tattoos. The pachucos spoke in a language that was a mix of Spanish and English. They represented a new culture among young people who were rebelling against their parents. In the past, many Mexican Americans had maintained strong, close-knit extended families, including parents, children, and grandparents. However, as more and more families moved into the cities, young people began to develop their own clothing styles, music, and language that separated them from the older generations.

On August 1, 1942, Enrique "Henry" Leyvas, a zoot-suiter, was parked with his girlfriend, Dora Barrios, at a reservoir called Sleepy Lagoon on a ranch outside of Los Angeles. There they were attacked and beaten up by a group of Mexican Americans. Afterward, Leyvas and Barrios gathered some of their friends and tried to find the young men who had attacked them. Eventually, they arrived at a nearby party, which the attackers had attended earlier. A fight began with the people who were still at the party. One of them, José Díaz, was killed. Díaz was 22 years old, a former employee at a vegetable packing plant who had recently enlisted in the armed forces to serve in World War II.

The following day, the police began arresting large numbers of young Mexican Americans, including Henry Leyvas, who were suspected of being involved in the killing. Leyvas and 21 other young men went on trial for the killing. Leyvas had a long history of run-ins with the police and had even gone to jail for assault. At the trial, which began in October, Leyvas was accused of being a gang leader who had turned other gang members on Díaz and his friends. The 22 young men had only seven lawyers to plead their case, which was not enough to provide them with a proper defense. Meanwhile, the judge made it clear throughout the trial that he disliked Leyvas and the others. They were portrayed in the newspapers as examples

Henry Leyvas was one of the zoot-suiters who were unfairly accused of murder in 1942.

of the criminal youth in the barrios. This portrayal was a stereo-type and was unfair to all the young people of the barrios. The trial ended in January 1943. Seventeen of the young men went to prison, including Leyvas, who was given a life sentence.

Shortly after the verdict was announced, leaders of the Mexican-American community formed the Sleepy Lagoon Defense Committee to get the verdict reversed. The committee received support from Hollywood stars, labor unions, and even members of Congress. It argued that the judge had been prejudiced against the young men because they were Mexican American and that they did not receive a fair trial. Eventually, the committee succeeded in obtaining a new trial. The verdict was overturned, and the young men were released from prison.

While the Sleepy Lagoon Defense Committee was working to get a new trial, another incident broke out in Los Angeles. Known as the Zoot Suit Riots of 1943, this conflict pitted soldiers against young Mexican Americans. The Anglo soldiers resented the young zoot-suiters who were not serving in the war. The zoot-suiters, in turn, resented the American soldiers who insulted them and tried to date Mexican young women.

On May 30, 1943, the two sides clashed. As a group of American soldiers and sailors walked toward some Mexican-American women, they were stopped by a group of zoot-suiters. A fight broke out, and the soldiers were driven off. On June 3, about 50 sailors invaded a theater and began beating up zoot-suiters. The next night, more soldiers and sailors stormed into Mexican-American neighborhoods. At first, the police did nothing to stop the riots. As one police officer said, "Many of us were in the First World War, and we're not going to pick on kids in the service." Instead, as the rioting grew worse, the police arrested young Mexican Americans. Finally, after a week of riots, President Roosevelt ordered military leaders to keep the soldiers and sailors on the bases and out of Los Angeles.

With that, the Zoot Suit Riots ended. However, they had clearly illustrated the serious problems faced by Mexican Americans. These issues would continue to affect Mexican immigrants after the end of World War II in 1945.

Opposite: Mexican American Cesar Chavez (in front) holds a sign during the successful 1968 grape boycott, which resulted in better wages for the vineyard workers, most of whom were fellow Mexicans.

Chapter Five

Mexican Immigrants and Civil Rights

A Struggle for Change

Veterans Fight Back

I n the three decades that followed World War II, Mexican Americans participated in a civil rights movement that changed the lives of immigrants of all backgrounds.

Some of these Mexican Americans were veterans of World War II. One such veteran was Hector Perez Garcia. Born in Mexico in 1914, Garcia was taken to the United States four years later by his parents, who were fleeing the violence of the Mexican Revolution. They settled with relatives in Texas, where Garcia's father helped manage a family business. Garcia graduated from the University of Texas, attended medical school, and enlisted in the army during World War II, winning the Bronze Star medal for bravery in battle. After the war, Garcia met his future wife, Wanda Fusillo, in Italy, and the couple returned to Texas to raise a family. Wanda Garcia was amazed at what she found there. "In Italy and many European countries . . . the word 'America' was always associated with liberty, equality and freedom of opportunity," she said. "I was dumbfounded [surprised] at the attitudes [of prejudice] displayed towards the Mexican people."

One incident stood out in her mind. In 1948, a Mexican-American soldier from Texas, Felix Longoria, was killed fighting the Japanese. Despite Longoria's service to his country, his family was not allowed to have a burial service or a cemetery plot in the town where he had grown up because they were Mexican. The Longoria family asked Garcia for help. Garcia contacted political leaders in Texas and in Washington, D.C. Finally, the Longoria family received permission for Felix to be buried in Arlington National Cemetery in Washington, D.C.

As a result of this incident, Garcia decided to start the GI Forum, aimed at Mexican-American former GIs, or members of the armed forces. This organization was committed to ending discrimination against Mexican Americans in Texas. Over the next decade, the GI Forum worked to end segregation in Texas schools and public places like swimming pools and movie theaters. Led by Garcia, the forum also became involved in politics, working to elect officials who would protect the rights of Mexican Americans.

Family members of Private Felix Longoria attend his funeral in Arlington National Cemetery, Virginia, in 1949.

Another organization committed to civil rights was the League of United Latin American Citizens (LULAC). Founded in Corpus Christi, Texas, in 1929, LULAC worked in states across the Southwest. In 1948, LULAC lawyers won a case that outlawed segregation in Texas schools. Nevertheless, many schools were slow to carry out the new law, prompting LULAC and the GI Forum to bring additional lawsuits against school districts throughout the 1950s. In 1954, LULAC won another case, which was presented in front of the United States Supreme Court. As a result of this case, Mexican Americans won the right to serve on juries.

Meanwhile, in California, the Community Service Organization (CSO) was campaigning to get Mexican Americans elected to public office. CSO leaders believed that if Mexican Americans achieved political power, they could reverse decades of discrimination. Candidates were elected to local school boards, and one Mexican American, Eduardo Roybal, became a member of the Los Angeles City Council in 1949.

Roybal, who had served in World War II, recalled:

> *In the army I was assigned to a barracks full of Texans. One of them woke up every morning and cursed Mexicans in general. Then one day he cursed me. So, I turned around and socked him. I knocked him out. That ended the argument right there. Most of us in the service had experiences like that. And then on the battlefield, every man was equal, of course. Death does not discriminate.*

Roybal and the other members of the CSO were committed to bringing the same equality to the United States.

Operation Wetback

Unfortunately, the work of political leaders such as Roybal came at a time when Mexican immigrants were receiving negative publicity in the news media. Bad economic conditions in Mexico were persuading poor Mexicans to travel to the United States. However, many of them crossed the border illegally. These immigrants were often called "wetbacks" because some of them supposedly swam across the Rio Grande, the river that marks the border between Mexico and the United States. In fact, most of these immigrants were brought across the border in trucks operated by the professional smugglers known as coyotes. These men were paid for bringing the immigrants past the U.S. Border Patrol. For $200, they even helped the illegal immigrants find jobs.

Immigration Laws

An immigration law passed in 1965 restricted the number of immigrants who could enter the United States from the Western Hemisphere to 120,000 per year. (The Western Hemisphere includes Mexico and Central and South America.) In 1977, a new law stated that only 20,000 immigrants from Mexico could legally cross the border per year. However, special circumstances pushed that number to 60,000 annually. Many Mexicans were allowed to enter as guest, or temporary, workers so they could work on farms.

In 1954, the U.S. government decided to crack down on the illegal immigration. In a program called Operation Wetback, more than a million of these immigrants were rounded up and sent back to Mexico. But this did not stop other immigrants from illegally entering the United States. Over the next two decades, more and more crossed the border and found homes in the barrios of large cities like Los Angeles. Between 1960 and 1975, 700,000 Mexican immigrants entered the United States legally, while an estimated 7 million crossed the border illegally. Often they went to work as fruit and vegetable pickers on large farms. The farm owners did not care whether their employees were legal or illegal immigrants, as long as they did the work. Indeed, the illegal status of many immigrants meant that they could not bargain for fair wages. If they asked for more money than the farm owners were willing to pay, the owners might report the illegal immigrants to the local authorities and have them sent back to Mexico.

An illegal immigrant attempts to enter the United States in 1954 in San Diego, California, by hiding in the hood of a car.

Illegal immigrants had none of the rights of American citizens. This meant that they could not vote in elections. As a result, Mexican-American leaders who were trying to increase support for their own politicians faced a difficult struggle. In addition, many Mexican Americans were poor and could neither read nor write English. They did not believe that the American political system, which was run by Anglos, had helped them in the past. They also did not believe that the political system could be changed. As a result, by the mid-1960s, there were only four Mexican Americans in the U.S. Congress. They included Eduardo Roybal of California, who was elected to the House of Representatives, and Joseph Montoya from New Mexico, the only Mexican-American senator in Congress.

The Chicano Movement

During the 1960s, minority groups in the United States began to press for the same rights enjoyed by the Anglo majority. African Americans, led by the Reverend Dr. Martin Luther King Jr., participated in civil rights marches and demonstrations to end school segregation, win the right to vote in elections, and achieve equality in the workplace. Instead of accepting their own position as second-class citizens, African Americans began to take great pride in their traditions and culture. At colleges and universities, students and teachers began participating in African studies programs. African-American poets, novelists, artists, and musicians also achieved greater recognition for their work.

A similar thing happened in the Mexican-American community. Known as the Chicano movement, it emphasized the positive aspects of Mexican tradition and encouraged Mexican Americans to take pride in their culture. Many young Mexican Americans believed that their leaders were going much too slowly in their quest for equality. Whether they were new immigrants themselves or the children of parents who had come to the United States decades earlier, Mexican Americans still faced the same problems.

MAPA

✿✿✿

One organization that worked to gain political power for Mexican Americans was the Mexican American Political Association (MAPA). Founded in 1960, MAPA was led by Eduardo Roybal and Bert Corona. Corona had been born in El Paso, Texas, in 1918. After his father was murdered, he was raised by his mother and grandmother. "They deplored [hated] any form of exploita-tion," he said, "and believed that people should instead conduct themselves in a humane, honest, and responsible manner." During the 1930s, Corona became a union organizer in Los Angeles and later worked with the CSO. In 1960, MAPA worked to organize Viva Kennedy Clubs in California to help elect John F. Kennedy president of the United States.

By the 1960s, Mexican Americans numbered more than 4 million. Nevertheless, fewer than 6 percent of them attended college, compared to 25 percent of the Anglo community. They earned, on average, only half as much as whites living in the United States. In addition, less than 5 percent were professionals such as doctors, lawyers, or teachers, compared to more than 15 percent of the white population. In the past, Mexican-American immigrants had often been content with their situation, since it seemed better than what they had experienced in Mexico. Many of them, hoping to return home to Mexico some day, viewed their lives in the United States as only temporary.

Younger Mexican Americans, however, saw things differ-ently. They viewed themselves as Americans, but they were not granted the same opportunities as the Anglos who lived in the United States. In schools, they were told to forget their Mexican heritage. If young people spoke Spanish in class, they were often punished. Most American schools stressed that children must learn English to succeed in society. While this probably made sense, it left Mexican Americans feeling inferior. "We look for others like ourselves in . . . history books," said a Mexican-American high school student from Los Angeles, "for something to be proud of for being a Mexican, and all we see in books, magazines, films, and TV shows are stereotypes of a dark, dirty, smelly man . . . [in] a big sombrero [hat]."

In 1968, Rodolfo "Corky" Gonzáles, one of the leaders of the Chicano movement, published a poem, "I Am Joaquín," which summed up the feelings of many Mexican Americans. In part, it reads:

> *I am Joaquín*
> *lost in a world of confusion*
> *caught up in the whirl of*
> *a gringo [white] society*
> *confused by the rules*
> *scorned by attitudes*
> *suppressed by manipulation*
> *and destroyed by modern society.*

Influential Chicano leader Rodolfo "Corky" Gonzáles (center) speaks at a conference at a state prison in Colorado in 1971.

Dolores Huerta

Cofounder of the UFW

Dolores Fernandez Huerta was born in Dawson, New Mexico, in 1930. Her mother encouraged Dolores to take piano lessons, sing in the church choir, and participate in the Girl Scouts. After her family moved to California, Huerta attended college and became a teacher. During the 1950s, she joined the CSO, where she met Cesar Chavez. She left the organization with him in 1961, and a year later they founded the UFW. During the strike at Delano, she walked the picket lines with the other workers and helped organize the successful grape boycott. She also led the fight for laws in California that allowed farmworkers to form a union and bargain with farm owners for fair wages.

During the 1960s, the leaders of the Chicano movement worked in a variety of areas to change the position of Mexican Americans in society. Perhaps the most famous of these leaders was Cesar Chavez. Born in 1927 in Arizona, Chavez worked as a farm laborer in California along with the other members of his family during the Great Depression. He served in the U.S. Navy during World War II. After the war, Chavez went back to work on a farm. He eventually joined the CSO and became one of its directors. However, Chavez soon realized that the CSO did not focus on the needs of farmworkers. Unable to convince the CSO to change its focus, he left the organization in 1961. A year later, he founded the United Farm Workers (UFW) with labor activist Dolores Huerta.

In 1965, a strike for higher wages broke out among farmworkers in vineyards in Delano, California. Chavez joined the strikers and gradually became their leader. A firm believer in the *huelga* (strike), Chavez hoped at first that he could persuade the vineyard owners to grant the strikers' demands for fair wages. However, the vineyards were owned by huge companies with seemingly unlimited money and power. Chavez eventually realized that the strike would not be enough to persuade these companies to bargain with him.

In 1968, Chavez organized a consumer boycott of grapes across the United States. As a result 17, million Americans refused to buy grapes. Chavez's boycott caused such a huge loss of business that in 1970 the grape growers finally agreed to recognize the UFW and negotiate with Chavez. This victory of the UFW led to the formation of other farmworker unions that staged strikes, led boycotts, and achieved new contracts.

Meanwhile, the Chicano movement had expanded into new areas. In the Southwest, Reies Tijerina led an effort among Mexican Americans to recover land that had been lost as a result of the U.S.-Mexican War in the 1840s. During the 1960s, Tijerina formed the Alianza Federal de Mercedes (Federal Alliance of Land Grants). In 1967, when Mexican Americans in New Mexico tried to hold a demonstration in support of the Alianza, they were arrested. Led by Tijerina, members of the Alianza broke into the courthouse to free the jailed demonstrators and kidnap the district attorney who had ordered the arrests. Gunfire broke out and two police officers were wounded. Tijerina was later brought to trial and eventually sent to prison in 1969. The Alianza was unsuccessful in obtaining any of the land grants.

During the late 1960s, college and high school students went on strike to protest segregation and call for more Mexican-American teachers in their classrooms. Students also demanded that schools begin offering bilingual education (education in two languages, such as English and Spanish). As a result, laws were passed requiring that classes be offered in Spanish as well as

English for Mexican-American and other Hispanic students. Bicultural education, which included Mexican history, also became a part of the public school curriculum. Chicano and Chicana (female Mexican American) programs were started at colleges and universities so students could learn about the contributions of Mexican-American political leaders, writers, and artists. These programs include the study of poets such as Corky Gonzáles, author of "I Am Joaquín," as well as stories drawn from the Indian and Spanish cultures of early Mexico.

In addition, the Chicano movement spurred other art forms. During the 1970s, Mexican-American artists painted large pictures, called murals, on the walls of buildings in barrios, in city parks, and in art galleries. Chicano musicians also became very popular. Singers such as Trinidad "Trini" Lopez recorded hit songs like "If I Had a Hammer" and "La Bamba."

Another art form that became popular during this period was the *teatro* (theater). During the 1960s, El Teatro Campesino (Farmworkers' Theater) was formed by Luis Valdez. The actors, who were farmworkers, put on performances for the strikers of the UFW as they walked the picket lines. After the strikes were over, the theater continued to put on plays that dealt with the struggles of Mexican Americans, as well as other themes. Valdez also continued to produce plays, including *Zoot Suit* in 1978, which was later turned into a film. The Farmworkers' Theater also led to the formation of other *teatros* that have become popular among American theatergoers.

As a result of the Chicano movement in the 1960s and 1970s, the lives of Mexican Americans underwent enormous changes in education, the arts, and the workplace. ▨

Opposite: *U.S. Border Patrol agents stand watch over a group of illegal immigrants after detaining them west of Laredo, Texas, in 2001.*

Chapter Six

Millions Cross the Border

Mexican Immigration in the Late 20th Century

A Huge Wave

Starting in the 1970s, huge numbers of Mexican immigrants began pouring into the United States. In 1980, the Mexican-American population stood at almost 9 million. By 1990, an additional 1.6 million Mexican immigrants had come to the United States, and the Mexican-American population reached more than 14 million people. (The fact that Mexican immigrants were having large families also contributed to the increase in the Mexican-American population.) The huge surge of people coming from Mexico to the United States continued over the next decade, with another 2.2 million crossing the border.

As it had been for most of the 19th and 20th centuries, the main force pushing so many immigrants from Mexico to the United States was poverty, while opportunities in the United States pulled Mexicans from their homeland. During the 1980s, poverty in Mexico increased greatly. While an estimated 32 million Mexicans lived in poverty in 1980, that number jumped to more than 42 million by the end of the decade. During the 1990s, the Mexican economy grew even worse. The Mexican peso—the currency used in Mexico, similar to the dollar—dropped in value. As a result, the money that Mexicans used was suddenly worth far less, and people could not afford to buy what they needed. By the mid-1990s, an estimated 80 percent of the Mexican population was living in poverty.

The majority of the poor lived in the cities, such as Mexico's capital, Mexico City. A severe earthquake there in 1985 made living conditions unbearable. As a result, thousands of Mexicans began heading north to the United States. Some were legal immigrants, but many others immigrated illegally. Among the immigrants were Native Americans, who often suffered from racial prejudice in Mexico. Many of them settled in Los Angeles, while others established new communities in Santa Monica and Oceanside, California. Other Native American immigrants went to Texas, where large groups settled in Houston.

What the Immigrants Found

M ost Mexican immigrants during this time settled in the Southwest, just as previous waves of Mexican immigrants had in the past. By the end of the 20th century, Los Angeles had the fourth-largest Mexican population in the world, greater than that of most cities in Mexico itself. The Mexican immigrant communities of several Texas cities, such as San Antonio, Corpus Christi, and El Paso, also continued to grow.

Like many before them, a large number of the Mexican immigrants of the late 20th century found themselves working in agricultural, or farming, jobs. Some new immigrants became migrant workers. They traveled from farm to farm throughout the United States, planting and picking produce, including sugar beets, onions, green beans, potatoes, apples, and cherries. They set up communities in North Carolina, where they picked tobacco, and in Florida, where they harvested oranges and other fruit. Others went north to New England to pick crops in the fall.

According to one estimate, there were 900,000 migrant workers in the United States in the 1990s. Most of them were Mexican men in their twenties. Migrant workers earned about $5,000 per year, which put them well below the national poverty line. (In 1995, an individual worker with an income of just under $8,000 per year was considered below the poverty line, meaning that he or she lived in poverty.) The migrant workers often left their families in Mexico and sent money home to support them, even though the workers had barely enough to take care of themselves. While living in the United States, the migrant workers could afford only cheap housing. Often a group of men lived together in a garage or a run-down shack.

Federico Ramos was one of these young men. In 1992 he left his mother and sister in Mexico and immigrated to the United States. First he traveled to California, then to Hermiston, Oregon, where his father lived. He found a job in the apple orchards as a farmworker. Ramos often put in long days during harvest time. "Sometimes you start early in the morning when the sun is coming up, [and work] until twelve [midnight, when] you can come home," he explained.

Many Mexican-American immigrants found work in food processing plants. This young woman is working in an apple factory.

In addition to the men who crossed the border, Mexican families also came north to work in the fields. According to one estimate, approximately 60 percent of the illegal immigrants were women. Children often worked side by side with their mothers in the fields. As a result, the children received little or no schooling.

Some Mexican immigrants of the late 20th century who started out as migrant workers were eventually fortunate enough to find jobs in food-processing plants. This year-round employment allowed migrant families to settle down and form communities. Towns in the Willamette River valley of Oregon and the Yakima River valley of Washington State developed large Mexican-American populations, which included former migrant workers.

Guadalupe Escobedo went to Umatilla, Oregon, in 1979, when she was 14 years old. She traveled there with her parents, who found jobs in a food-processing plant. After going to school most of the year, Guadalupe worked in the fields. "I . . . weeded watermelon, weeded carrots, weeded onions," she said. "I worked on the machine that had the plastic bags for the potatoes. . . . I operated the machine . . . stapled the bags, and I sorted potatoes." But Guadalupe had no intention of spending the rest of her life as a farmworker. She attended college in Sacramento, California. After returning to Oregon and working at a community health clinic, Escobedo realized that she was really drawn to teaching. At first she taught young children in Sunday school. "I liked the feeling of teaching kids and talking to kids and being around them," she explained. She went back to school to become a teacher. Today she teaches first grade in Hermiston, Oregon.

Other Mexican immigrants traveled to the central part of the United States, settling in Kansas. They followed earlier groups of Mexicans who had gone to Kansas at the beginning of the century to work in railroad construction. During the 1970s and 1980s, the immigrants worked in Kansas's meatpacking industry. By the end of the 20th century, Mexicans had become the fastest-growing immigrant group in the state. Mexican Americans began to settle in other areas of the Midwest as well.

German Pantoja, for example, left central Mexico to work on a farm in Indiana and was later hired at a factory. He and his wife Irma, another Mexican immigrant, began baking cookies and breads at home and selling them to workers at the factory. In 2000, they opened their own bakery. "I've never had my own business," Irma said. "This seemed like something impossible, but little by little, we are doing it. We are making a living together."

In addition to the many poor people, like German and Irma Pantoja, who left Mexico, middle-class Mexicans also immigrated to the United States. These included businesspeople from Mexico City who had been laid off from their jobs due to the poor Mexican economy. Skilled workers, such as electricians and carpenters, also headed north because they could not find jobs in Mexico. Some of them were able to open shops and establish small businesses in the United States.

Mexican-American Influence

As Mexican immigrants settled in large numbers in the northwestern United States in the last decades of the 20th century, they brought their cultural traditions with them. The immigrants formed theater groups that put on Mexican plays. Mexican-American girls looked forward to their Quinceañera, a special celebration held when a girl turns 15 to mark the fact that she has become an adult. Some immigrants opened taquerias—Mexican fast-food restaurants—as well as *tortillerias*, or tortilla factories. Other Mexican Americans went into service businesses that provided lawn care and landscaping. Spanish-language newspapers and radio and television programs began to appear. As the Mexican-American population increased elsewhere around the United States, immigrants brought the same traditions to their new communities.

Federico Peña, formerly the mayor of Denver, Colorado, was secretary
of transportation and secretary of energy in the 1990s.

Success in Many Fields

As the Mexican-American population increased, Mexican Americans became more and more visible in American society. Some Mexican Americans entered politics at the local, state, and national levels. Federico Peña, for example, was born in Texas in 1947 and became a lawyer during the 1970s. In 1983 he was elected mayor of Denver, Colorado. Ten years later, President Bill Clinton appointed Peña as secretary of transportation. President Clinton also appointed Mexican American Henry Cisneros to his cabinet, as secretary of housing and urban development. Cisneros had served as mayor of San Antonio from 1981 to 1989, and was the first Mexican American to become the mayor of a large city. Another Mexican-American political leader is Gloria Molina, a daughter of immigrants. She was the first Chicana to be a member of the California state legislature and the Los Angeles City Council, where she has served since 1991.

Mexican Americans have also distinguished themselves in professional sports. Born in 1939, golfer Lee Trevino was raised by his mother and grandfather. At age five, he went to work picking cotton to help support his family. "I thought hard work was just how life was," he said. Trevino began caddying (carrying equipment for golfers) on golf courses when he was eight years old, and he started practicing his golf shots. Eventually, Trevino joined the

Lee Trevino

Professional Golfers' Association (PGA) tour, twice winning three of its major events, the U.S. Open, the British Open, and the PGA Championship. Another highly successful Mexican-American golfer is Nancy Lopez, winner of 48 events on the Ladies' Professional Golf Association Tour and a member of the golf Hall of Fame. Commenting on Lopez's outstanding athletic skills, another golfer said: "She plays by feel. All her senses come into play. That's when golf is an art."

The arts are another area in which many Mexican Americans have made significant contributions. Since the 1980s, they have created what some have called the Chicano Renaissance. Among the writers who have been part of this renaissance is Tomás Rivera. Born in Texas in 1935 to migrant farmworkers, Rivera became a university professor. Some of his novels, poetry, and short stories, including "The Harvest" (published in 1989), describe the lives of migrant workers.

Unlike Rivera, Lucha Corpi was born in Mexico, but went to California and attended college. As Corpi explains, her books "study all forms of racism" against Mexican Americans. Her first book of poetry, *Noon Words,* published in 1980, was followed by a novel, *Delia's Song,* in 1989, which describes the experiences of a Chicana during the civil rights movement of the 1960s. Corpi published another book of poems, *Variations on a Storm,* in 1990, followed by several mystery stories.

Sandra Cisneros is a Chicana writer who explores the role of women in Mexican-American society. Although Cisneros's parents were poor, they insisted that Sandra and her siblings go to college so they could be successful. "My father's hands are thick and yellow," she said, "stubbed by a history of hammer and nails. . . . 'Use this,' my father said, tapping his head, 'not this,' showing us those hands." During the 1980s and 1990s, Cisneros published novels, poems, and short stories. One of her best-known works, published in 1984, is *The House on Mango Street.* It describes the life of a Mexican-American girl, Esperanza Cordero, in a Chicago barrio. Cordero eventually leaves the barrio, but a friend tells her, "You will always be Esperanza. You will always be Mango Street. You can't erase what you know. You can't forget who you are."

As well-established Mexican Americans continued to put their stamp on American culture, new immigrants poured across the border from Mexico.

NAFTA and Immigration

In 1994, conditions in Mexico grew worse than ever. Officials from Mexico, the United States, and Canada signed the North American Free Trade Agreement (NAFTA). The purpose of NAFTA was to eventually eliminate the tariffs (taxes) that each country had to pay on goods that came from the other two nations. For example, all tariffs on farm products were to be eliminated. Mexican farmers were hopeful that this would create a large market in the United States where they could sell their products.

But the farmers were disappointed. Instead of creating more markets for Mexican goods, NAFTA had the effect of flooding the Mexican market with lower-priced American farm products. Mexican farmers could not compete with the lower prices of U.S. farm products, so they were unable to sell their own products. As a result, many Mexican farmers were forced to leave their land. Most went to large Mexican cities looking for jobs. At first, many found jobs thanks to another effect of NAFTA. The farmers may not have been able to export, or send, their products to the United States, but manufacturers found a huge market there for their goods, such as clothing. New factories called maquiladoras sprang up in northern Mexico, near the U.S. border. The maquiladoras supplied cheap products for the export market. The main reason these products were so cheap was that Mexican workers were paid far less than similar employees in the United States.

But the manufacturing jobs created by NAFTA were not to last. By the beginning of the 21st century, the U.S. economy was struggling. More people lost their jobs and were not buying as many manufactured goods. As a result, many Mexicans were also laid off from their jobs. They began looking northward for employment. Even with a weak economy, the United States still seemed more promising than Mexico. As one immigrant put it: "If you're going to improve your life, you have to go to the United States."

Opposite: *Today's Mexican Americans are found at all levels of society. While many still work as laborers, more and more are educated professionals, such as this optometrist.*

Chapter Seven

Overcoming the Challenges

Mexican Immigrants Today

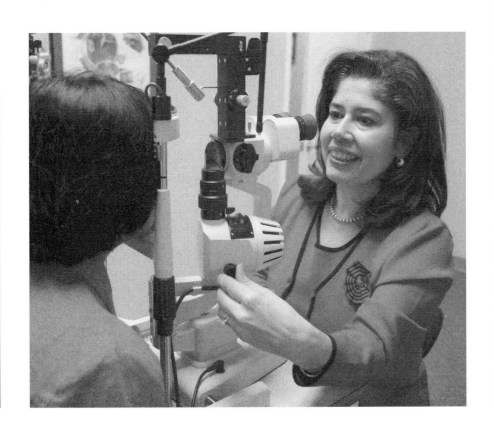

The New Immigrants

During the first few years of the 21st century, an estimated 350,000 Mexicans were legally entering the United States each year. Hundreds of thousands more crossed the border illegally. Mexicans continued to form America's largest immigrant group. Meanwhile, the population of Mexican Americans had grown to more than 21 million. As they have throughout history, most live in the Southwest, a geographical area that Mexican Americans call Aztlán, or the homeland. Like so many before them, many of these immigrants crossed the border to escape the poor economy in Mexico, hoping to find economic opportunity in the United States. What they found was hope, as well as despair.

Most Mexican immigrants have settled in these states.

*Because of discrimination in the workplace, many Mexican Americans
are employed in low-paying jobs, like this young man who is cleaning
and packing jicamas, a potato-like food.*

Encountering Prejudice

S ome of the Mexican immigrants entering the United States
today, as well as those who came during the last decades of
the 20th century, continue to encounter prejudice from American
citizens who regard them as unwelcome newcomers. These
Americans include people of all races—even Mexican Americans
who have already established themselves in the United States.
These Mexican Americans fear that the new immigrants will
work for less money, causing wages to be lowered for everyone
eventually. When new immigrant Antonio Perez took a job at a

meatpacking plant in Kansas, he discovered that his Mexican-American supervisors looked down on him. "Go back to Mexico, wetback," they told him. Indeed, the influx of Mexican Americans has had the effect of lowering wages among immigrant populations.

As new Mexican immigrants arrive in the Midwest and Southwest, where Mexican-American communities were established long ago, some Mexican Americans who have lived there for several generations are upset. They have worked to fit into American society, and over time they have been accepted. However, the presence of the new immigrants threatens to change the situation by creating new tensions between Mexican Americans and other groups. Some native-born Americans fear that, in addition to lowering wages, the arrival of more Mexican Americans will mean an increase in the number of children in the schools, and therefore higher taxes.

New Laws

This fear has resulted in changes to the law. In California, for example, citizens were concerned that the large number of Mexican immigrants, both legal and illegal, would greatly increase the costs of government services. After all, these immigrants sent their children to public schools and used local hospitals. In 1994, citizens voted to pass a law called Proposition 187. This law stated that illegal immigrants could not use these services. In 1998, however, a U.S. federal judge struck down most of the law, saying that it was unconstitutional (it went against the Constitution of the United States). That same year, California voters passed Proposition 227, which ended most bilingual education programs. A similar law was passed in Arizona in 2000. Many Americans, including some Mexican Americans, believe that non-English-speaking immigrant children should be placed in English-speaking classrooms so they can learn how to compete in American society as soon as possible.

Indeed, some experts believe that the inability of some Mexican Americans to speak fluent English prevents them from succeeding in the United States. Currently, barely 50 percent of Mexican-American students graduate from high school. As a result, many can find only low-paying jobs and are forced to live in poverty.

People of Color

Some Mexican immigrants face severe discrimination because of their skin color. Many mestizos, for example, who are descendants of Native Americans and Spaniards, have fairly dark skin. Even though many of them live in areas that have very large Mexican-American populations, such as Los Angeles and El Paso, they encounter discrimination. Researchers found that mestizos suffer more discrimination than any other Mexican Americans or Mexican immigrants in general. They are more likely to be victims of housing segregation (meaning that they are often forced to live separately from others), and they are more poorly represented in the government. The researchers also point out that this discrimination occurs not because mestizos are Mexican and speak English with an accent but because of their skin color.

The Effects of Proposition 227

Proposition 227, passed in 1998, still has many supporters and opponents. Its supporters point to an improvement in test scores among California students. From 1998 to 2000, reading scores increased by 35 percent, math scores increased by 43 percent, and spelling scores improved by 44 percent.

According to supporters, these improvements show that it is better for all students to learn in English. However, opponents of Proposition 227 point to other statistics showing that test scores increased for all students—not just Mexican immigrants—as teachers increased their ability to prepare students to take the tests. Test scores for all students had improved again by 2002, but critics claim that all this proves is that teachers were even better at teaching their students to take the tests.

The critics do not see these improved scores as proof that students are actually learning more. In addition, critics point out, the law has had little effect on the numbers of Mexican immigrant students improving from beginning English to more advanced levels. Only 7.8 percent of immigrant children became fluent in English in 2002. In 1998, before Proposition 227 took effect, that number was 7 percent. Proposition 227's opponents say that the law is unfair and that it is not making a difference.

Illegal Immigrants

If life in the United States is often difficult for Mexican immigrants in general, it can seem impossible at times for those who are in the country illegally. Illegal immigrants have no rights as U.S. citizens. This makes them easy targets for dishonest employers, who hire them for many reasons. One reason is that the immigrants are desperate for jobs and will work for very low wages. And because they are illegal immigrants, they are afraid to protest against low pay or unfair treatment lest their employers report them to government authorities. By hiring illegal immigrants, for example, fruit and vegetable growers can avoid paying the higher wages of union workers who belong to the United Farm Workers. As a result, union membership has declined. Illegal immigrants generally do not join unions because they do not want their names to become known and to be reported to the authorities.

A U.S. Border Patrol agent drives along the border separating Mexico and the United States near Jacumba, California, as men wait on the Mexican side before attempting an illegal crossing.

Illegal immigrants are also hired by contractors who find jobs for them with local merchants. In 2003, federal agents found illegal immigrants working at large Wal-Mart department stores as cleaners. Wal-Mart managers claimed they did not know that the immigrants were illegal, because Wal-Mart had hired the workers through contractors. Wal-Mart also claimed to be unaware that the contractors were not paying the workers extra for overtime and that the contractors were not paying taxes to the government. Companies such as Wal-Mart hire illegal immigrants "for the same reason they've always done it, to save money," said a lawyer who deals with employment issues. "These companies are pretending they're not the employer. The contractor is willing to work people seven days a week, [and] not pay . . . taxes. . . . The companies don't want to do that themselves, but they're willing to look the other way when their contractors do it." Dishonest employers take advantage of the desperate situation of illegal Mexican immigrants, who have no rights under the law. Many immigrants, however, are willing to take these risks for the chance of a better life in the United States.

Mexicans Give Back

The prejudice and discrimination faced by Mexican immigrants is only part of their story. Wherever Mexican Americans have established communities, they have brought along their customs, culture, and traditions. Most are proud to be living and working in the United States. Even so, they have not forgotten the people and places they left behind in Mexico, and many work hard to help those in their homeland. Each year, Mexican immigrants send an estimated $14.5 billion to families back home. According to one expert, this money assists 25 million people in Mexico to pay for food, housing, and schools.

Some Mexican immigrants have established organizations just for this purpose. Members of a thriving community of Mexican immigrants in the Bronx, a section of New York City, collect small contributions and send them back to their hometowns in Mexico. Avenamar Cruz, for example, came to the United States from Atopoltitlan, Mexico. Along with other immigrants from the same town, Cruz has contributed money that has been used to pay for festivals, build basketball courts, and install streetlights in Atopoltitlan. Nicholás Sánchez, another Mexican-American New Yorker, came to the United States from San Miguel Comitlipa. He has not forgotten the needs of the people back home and sends money to improve his former community. "I can do something for the place where I was born," he said. "It makes you feel good, like you have a purpose."

Like Cruz and Sánchez, most Mexican immigrants and established Mexican-American families do not forget who they are or where they came from. These immigrants combine rich traditions from the past with the experience of living in the United States to make a unique contribution to American culture.

President Bush, left, presents Mexican-American writer Rudolfo Anaya with a National Medal of Arts Award in 2002.

Speaking Spanish

Here are a few words of Spanish origin that have become a familiar part of the English language. Many of them originated in Mexico.

bronco: a wild horse or pony found in western North America

macho: a strong and sometimes exaggerated sense of masculinity

mesa: flat, raised, tablelike land with steep cliffs on all sides

nacho: tortilla chip topped with cheese, chili sauce, and other toppings

patio: a roofless courtyard attached to a house

pinto: a horse with large spotted markings

poncho: a blanketlike cape with a hole in the center that fits over the head

pronto: quickly, without delay

renegade: an outlaw or rebel who rejects established authority

rodeo: an exhibition of bronco riding, cattle roping, and other similar activities

siesta: an afternoon nap often taken after the midday meal

A New Spirit

Mexican immigrants have been coming to the area that is the United States since before the American Revolution. Over the past four centuries, they have enriched American culture with Mexican traditions, including art, festivals, literature, and ethnic foods. Today, they bring a new sense of purpose and a new spirit to the United States. Mexican immigrants play many important roles in American society. One of the most important is to remind other Americans, many of whose ancestors were immigrants themselves, that hard work and determination can still mean success, just as they have for generations.

Time Line of Mexican Immigration

1519 Hernán Cortés lands in Mexico, begins conquest of Aztec.

1598 Juan de Oñate establishes settlement in New Mexico.

1610 Settlement established by Spanish at Santa Fe, New Mexico.

1680 Pueblo Rebellion led by Native Americans erupts in New Mexico.

1680s Father Eusebio Kino begins establishing missions in Arizona.

1692–1694 Spanish defeat Native Americans and take back control of New Mexico.

1718 Spanish establish presidio and mission at San Antonio, Texas.

1769 Presidio and mission established at San Diego, California.

1776 Spanish establish presidio at Tucson, Arizona.

1803 United States makes Louisiana Purchase.

1821 Mexico becomes independent from Spain.

1835–1836 Texas wins independence from Mexico.

1846–1848 United States acquires Arizona, New Mexico, and California from Mexico as a result of winning U.S.-Mexican War.

1853 United States makes Gadsden Purchase, acquiring land on Mexico's northern border.

1880s–1910 Dictator Porfirio Díaz leads Mexico.

1900–1930 About 1.5 million Mexicans flee Mexico for the United States.

1930s During the Great Depression, 400,000 Mexican immigrants return to Mexico.

1942 Bracero Program begins, bringing thousands of Mexican immigrants into United States.

1942–1945	In World War II, 12 Mexican Americans win Congressional Medal of Honor.
1943	Zoot Suit Riots break out in Los Angeles.
1954	U.S. government launches Operation Wetback.
1960	Mexican American Political Association (MAPA) founded.
1960s–1970s	Chicano movement emphasizes pride in Mexican-American culture.
1961	Cesar Chavez and Dolores Huerta found the United Farm Workers Union (UFW).
1970	The UFW is recognized by large agricultural companies following a long boycott.
1980–1990	Increasing numbers of Mexicans enter United States.
1984	Chicana writer Sandra Cisneros publishes her novel *The House on Mango Street*.
1990	U.S. Border Patrol tries to reduce number of illegal immigrants from Mexico.
1990–2000	2.2 million Mexican immigrants arrive.
1993	President Bill Clinton appoints Mexican Americans as members of his cabinet.
1994	Officials from Mexico, the United States, and Canada sign the North American Free Trade Agreement (NAFTA). This results in a loss of work for Mexican farmers.
	Proposition 187 is passed in California. The law says that illegal immigrants are not eligible for government benefits such as welfare.
2000	Legal immigration from Mexico is 350,000 annually.
2003	Federal officials bring attention to the problem of companies hiring illegal-immigrant workers and not paying or treating them fairly.

*Sammy McClure MS
Media Center*

Glossary

barrio Mexican-American neighborhood in a city.

bilingual Using or able to use two languages.

Californio Mexican person living in California during the 18th and 19th centuries.

coyote Professional smuggler who helps Mexicans cross the U.S. border illegally.

culture The language, arts, traditions, and beliefs of a society.

emigrate To leave one's homeland to live in another country.

ethnic Having certain racial, national, tribal, religious, or cultural origins.

fiesta Party, celebration.

hacienda Large farm or ranch in a Spanish-speaking area.

immigrate To come to a foreign country to live.

mestizo Person living in Mexico of mixed Indian and Spanish heritage.

migrant worker Laborer who travels from one location to the next doing jobs.

prejudice Negative opinion formed without just cause.

presidio Garrison, or fort, of Spanish troops.

refugee Someone who flees a place for safety reasons, especially to another country.

segregation Separation of groups of people from each other, especially according to race.

stereotype Simplified and sometimes insulting opinion or image of a person.

Further Reading

BOOKS

Behnke, Alison. *Mexicans in America.* Minneapolis: Lerner, 2004.

Bloom, Barbara Lee. *The Mexican Americans.* San Diego, Cal.: Gale Group, 2003.

Catalano, Julie. *The Mexican Americans.* New York: Chelsea House, 1988.

Del Castillo, Richard Griswold, and Arnoldo De Leon. *North to Aztlan: A History of Mexican Americans in the United States.* New York: Twayne, 1997.

Gnojewski, Carol. *Cinco de Mayo: Celebrating Hispanic Pride.* Berkeley Heights, N.J.: Enslow, 2002.

Perl, Lila. *North across the Border: The Story of the Mexican Americans.* New York: Benchmark Books, 2002.

WEB SITES

Los Culturas.com. "Mexican-American Culture." URL: http://www.lasculturas.com/lib/libMexico.php. Downloaded on August 18, 2004.

Puro Mariachi. "History of the Mariachi." URL: http://www.mariachi.org/history.html. Updated on June 11, 2004.

San Diego Historical Society. "Education Program." URL: http://www.sandiegohistory.org/education/education.htm. Updated on June 11, 2004.

United Farm Workers (UFW). "The Story of Cesar Chavez." URL: http://www.ufw.org/cecstory.htm. Updated on June 11, 2004.

Index